Livid,
Lucid,
Lust

Livid, Lucid, Lust

Janet Saltzman

LIVID, LUCID, LUST

iUniverse books may be ordered through booksellers or by contacting:

iUniverse
1663 Liberty Drive
Bloomington, IN 47403
www.iuniverse.com
844-349-9409

ISBN: 978-1-6632-2065-3 (sc)
ISBN: 978-1-6632-2066-0 (e)

Print information available on the last page.

iUniverse rev. date: 04/01/2021

Contemporary society believes more in
what they hear than what they see
People believe in lip more than literature This
gives new meaning to "I can't believe my eyes"
@gpc

Oh Lord here I sit
Amongst all this evil
And beg, dear Lord to deliver me from it
@gpc

If they speak of others to you
They speak of you to others
@gpc

Janet Saltzman

Anyone who walks around
Thinking they're the smartest person
Is the dumbest person
Because they've learned nothing else
@gpc

Women in Vain

Unlike feminists
The poor little "mes"
Who want to get paid the same as he
And all the while the manipulating
winers get cheese and grapes
While us feminits work alongside the apes
and because of the poor little "mes"
We get called names
@gpc

When we go out you say "shut up and make you look good"
Well that's a moment for you to savor
Cause at the same time and at the same
moment i feel like a party favor
My name won't be etched at your toes
I won't be covered in fake brass
I'm allergic to fake gold
@gpc

I prefer to chop off my legs To lend a
helping hand Before using my feet
To step on everyone else
Just to help myself
@gpc

Put it down
Your swinging your sword in air When
no one is fighting you Put it down
@gpc

All that you express
Won't bring you happiness If you seek its
acceptance From everyone else
@gpc

I've been hurt, broken, used
And abused Yet I still refuse To be moved
@gpc

Any man who cannot stand by his word
Cannot stand by me
@gpc

Janet Saltzman

Pray for the world
Ans weep for the wicked
@gpc

Come forth
One who is
More noble than true
@gpc

Janet Saltzman

If I seem a strange girl
Just to you
I strange to others too For me it's nothing new Think I'm
weird and odd For what I say and do Maybe it's cause
I got a few screws that's loose
@gpc

Trusting my company
Is getting rough
I keep getting screwed
By now it should've made me tough
@gpc

Don't be afraid to speak the truth
They'll turn it all around You know they do When your word
Gets back to you
It turns into a story that's news to you
@gpc

When you speak your mind
They think your rude
The way they take it
I don't care
Do you
Make mountains out of mole hills is what they do
They can stick their mountains and their mole hills to
@gpc

If you believe in thoughts and opinions Delivered
through racist hatred What you think and say is mute
Because you're easily manipulated
@gpc

If someone always tells you
Something bad Don't believe it Defy it
@gpc

What was that you said
There's so many people talking in my head
Everyone's talking at once
I'd wish they'd all just shut up They don't give me
no kind of peace So I can put my mind at ease
@gpc

Every time I try to do
Something good
I end up getting bit in the ass
So now I do Something bad For a good reason
@gpc

Janet Saltzman

There may be no way
To excuse me
But there's no way to excuse you
From what you do
@gpc

Everytime I say "I've learned"
Everything that has befallen me
I've earned
@gpc

Look deep inside One thing you'll find There
will be a time You will rationalize
That we name and label
What we don't understand
Overload of info at hand To you it will make sense
Our decision we defend Because we take offense
Blame it on the seven deadly sins
@gpc

Can't focus just cry Tears fill my eyes On the screen
It seems
I'm unable to write
@gpc

Why do I keep doing it?
The same thing keeps happening
It's making me livid When will it
stop? Wait! Now that's what
I am the drug, this I have Nothing will
control me Especially anything bad
For this I am blessed and glad
@gpc

They say "I'm so nice to you" This can't be true
Say what you want to hear to get something from you
Being nice to get it to
Is what they do
This game makes me sad
If I do the same
It makes me feel bad
@gpc

For the life of me
I can't figure out the why
In a lie
@gpc

When much becomes too much
Demons want you to give up
Enough is enough
When much becomes too much Demons want
you to give up Well, enough is enough
I shan't stop or give up
@gpc

Janet Saltzman

Why do I have to stay strong? I've no shoulders to lean on
@gpc

Make up your own story
It is easy
To cause misery
Between you and me Whatever makes you
happy, baby Contradictory, to me
Apparently, in your speech
Can't even understand what you say to me
Fool of me to believe
But not asked of thee Promises made that
you don't keep Call it a mystery
Why support me?
@gpc

Why do I help everyone else
When I need help myself
When I need help No one hears me yell When I'm down
They don't stick around
When I need help
No one can be found
@gpc

Society tries to make me
Live their ways
Or they'll break me
Society lets me speak my mind
Until they find it unkind
@gpc

WHY ARE YOU YELLING!?
Do you think no one can hear you?
Stop raising your voice No one is
listening to you Because you're
YELLING!
@GPC

Your thoughts and opinions
are your own
Tell the the lippy cow down the road
To go home
If you believe in their opinions and thoughts
The value in your own
No one, will have not
@gpc

Janet Saltzman

I check my inventory
I rake my own backyard
Don't tell me about mine
And I won't tell you about yours
@gpc

Don't go looking in your neighbors yard
Before mowing your own lawn
@gpc

For so long
It's been so wrong I've been to crazy And when I got back
All I got was a T-shirt and a hat
Now I'm going insane And I've got no
one else But myself to blame
So leave me alone
Let me go on
Cause I'm trying to get back
Everything I had Cause crazy took that For so long
It's been so wrong
@gpc

What you don't understand
Will you explain it away
If you can
@gpc

To summarize
You realize
You don't have a name For things you
can't explain Don't file it away
Accept it all the same
@gpc

Something that you said from the start
Why do we have to be so far apart?
@gpc

Janet Saltzman

Sometimes I have to ask people
If they come with a note
If they actually answer me
Then batteries weren't included
@gpc

Men always say that women shop too
long and spend too much money
Men walk into a store
And in less time
Spend the same Amount of money
Buying top of the line

They are not happy
Until you are not Happy
@gpc

The public produces Piddly
Putrid people
@gpc

Some people feel the Pain
Others just cry about it
@gpc

We've signed a Social Contract
Based on a Harm Principle
To have our life, liberty, and private property
protected by the same people who are violating our
life, liberty, and private property to harm us.

Our justice system is like Swiss cheese
One part of our rights has to leave
The other has to give
Because someone gets too sensitive
@gpc

Oh My Dear Shakespeare, Upon Me Prov'd

Oh my dear Shakespeare
I shan't e'er say you are mistaken
But love is not love should anyone be forsaken
Love cannot be some kiss on rosy cheeks But love can be
fake from the lips that it leaves No love's not time's fool
Over time, it's love, it is love that you lose
And love cannot heal old wounds Only music can
calm "The Savage Beast" But love, not love, not
love in the least Yes, love is an ever-fixed mark
Like a scar on a broken heart
Yes love can be the light that leads every lost sailor home
But only if love leads you to that special someone
Lest I not forget from the tot of 16, I knew Before
you love someone else, you must love you
Oh my dear Shakespeare I shan't e'er say you are mistaken
But love is not love
Should anyone be forsaken
@gpc

Janet Saltzman

As a female I stand alone
My personal property on display
But for no one to own
@gpc

It is someone else who bears us
It's someone else who rears us Its someone else
who raises us It's someone else who praises
us It's someone else who teaches us
It's someone else who reaches us It's someone else
who hires us It's someone else who fires us
It's someone else who loves you It's someone
else who says "I do" When we die
It is someone else who puts down to lie So why
not think of someone else While we are alive
@gpc

If you don't say anything
It's all for nothing
@gpc

I didn't change my personality
I changed my person
I still did things my way
I just changed my ways
@gpc

Janet Saltzman

We've signed a social contract
To have our life, liberty, and private property protected
By the very ones who are violating it
@gpc

When talking at the same time
Doesn't matter what is said
Or how it matters how it's delivered
@gpc

If children are to be seen and not heard
I'm scared
Because children are our future If the meek
is to inherit the earth I'm scared
Don' t the good die young If cheaters
never prosper I'm scared
Why do good guys finish last
If too many cooks spoil the broth
I'm scared
Why are two heads better than one
If the past shapes our future
I'm scared
Why do we not learn from our mistakes If mankind
has dominion over the earth I'm scared
Mankind is destined for destruction If we wine
that things are never easy I'm scared
Why do we wine things are too good to be true
@gpc

Utilitarianism: That smile that is so
memorable and contagious
Thank you for always making my day so special
All the hard work you put into each day
to put others ahead of yourself
You are truly a remarkable individual
Every person is extremely lucky to cross paths with
your charismatic positive influences you add to
the lives you touch each and every day For that,
I thank you from the bottom of my heart
@CD

Janet Saltzman

Doesn't it seem woeful
To wilt away such wonder
@gpc

We can't solve a problem
If we are part of the problem
It's like being a room
With the same smell We don't notice it Because we're
living in it That's why we can't see The part we play in it
@gpc

My wonderful Canada
Which loves
Nothing but hellos and hugs
@gpc

A kind word
May be a short statement
But it goes a long way
@gpc

Janet Saltzman

A wise tongue
Is stronger and sharper
Than a pen or sword
@gpc

Violence begets violence
Use your head instead
@gpc

Use your mouth And mind Nothing else
@gpc

If you find yourself in loneliness And longing
for something else Don't you distress
There's someone else
I found him in myself And what dropped
my jaws He forgave my flaws
Now I plainly see
I wasn't flying with the eagles
I was running with the turkeys

If you're in a place
Full of dispute and hate
Just let them speak their peace
Don't worry about them Screaming and
shouting Put your mind at ease
If all they do
Is argue with you
Only he can make them see They're not flying with
the eagles They're running with the turkeys

If you just sit down
Take a look around
Can you trust the friends you've found
Is he one of them
You can trust in Him Cause He won't
let you down If you find one day
You don't have any faith Just get down on
your knees Raise your hands up
And say "Jesus"
I'm not flying with the eagles
I'm just running with the turkeys
@gpc

Being part of something
Greater than yourself Is a feeling greater Than anything else
@gpc

Complacency of where you're at
Were you good at where you sat
@gpc

Janet Saltzman

Just knowing
You can go without it
Will give you Enough confidence to Do without it
@gpc

Indignance to what you want
Shows no appreciation for what you have
@gpc

Janet Saltzman

Soldiers of us are made a few Altruistic
characteristics is what is asked of you
@gpc

Please do not place external blame
Own your truth
@gpc

Janet Saltzman

Women hate each other over materialism and men
But don't that together we are stronger than both
@gpc

Wisdom comes from opening a book
Not your mouth
We should believe more in literature
Than lip
@gpc

Janet Saltzman

Proper preparation Prevents poor Performance
@gpc

To be young
Don't think it
Or act it
Just feel it
@gpc

Janet Saltzman

Only the house broken
Can teach the paper trained
You have to have gone through it
To help those who are going through it
@gpc

Livid, Lucid, Lust

2 do, 2 day
2 nite, 2mrw
4 me, 4 now
4 ward, 4 ever
@gpc

Janet Saltzman

We've the opportunity
To be so much more
Why be like everyone else
@gpc

Questions you're afraid to ask
Can never be answered
If you find it a task
To look within yourself
And nowhere else
@gpc

Janet Saltzman

I try to explain
My dreamscape livid My nightmares lucid My situation vivid
My REM doesn't change a thing But continues
when I sleep again It's a sequel
Nightscapes are livid When I awake
I'm lucid My dreams are vivid
All dreams I remember
A curse I wish I can turn to ember
@gpc

I know I am just
I live my ways
By what Christ says
And in God I trust
@gpc

Those who live in wrath and revenge
Who use their offspring To bully your
offspring With no recompense
Live with no self confidence
@gpc

Oh Lord, I'm ready to die
I've wasted the times
Important in life
Oh Lord, I beg plead and cry
Oh Lord, I'm not ready to die

Oh Lord, I'm ready to die There's so
much in life That I didn't try
Oh Lord, just a little more time
Oh Lord, I'm not ready to die

Oh Lord, I'm ready to die I've had so
much fun But it just ain't enough
Oh Lord, doesn't time fly
Oh Lord, I'm not ready to die

Oh Lord, I'm not ready to die
I want to do what is right
To lead a good life
Oh Lord, just one more try
Oh Lord, I'm not ready to die

Oh Lord, I'm not ready to die
I beg plead and cry For a little more time Doesn't time fly
Just one more try
Oh Lord, I'm not ready to die
@GPC

Janet Saltzman

I know you can
Don't tell you can't
I know you will
Don't tell me you won't I've faith in what
you can do Don't tell me you don't
@gpc

If you drink So not to think In the end
It's just pretend
You can't run from your problems They'll appear
again and again You have to solve them
There's no garbage bag that big So you got
your chance to get away Did you need that
temporary vaca While in your state of mind
Was it a great escape
Did you meet new friends along the way Remember
the promises you made Now that you came down
Did your problems go away?
@gpc

Appreciate the things you are handed
These things others demand it The true meaning
of this situation Is that some are mistaken
To take this literally
In that, is the travisty Appreciating, is taking the
situation mentally Some don't get these things at all
@gpc

You have debts to pay
Try as you may
To hide away From the mistakes That you've made
You'll have debts to pay
@gpc

Oh, how nice Bright my life, would
be To have a friend like me
No matter flaws that surface Who'd
say, it's ok Nobody's perfect
Even when I'm not in the room
Me, you will defend
One who'll speak the truth
Even if I take offense One on whom I
can depend Until the very end
How nice it would be
You as a friend to me
@gpc

I'm afraid of being fed up Because I don't do
something I'm fed up of being afraid
So now I'm going to do something
@gpc

Good things come to those who wait
But not to those who procrastinate
@gpc

Beg your pardon
I thought I heard you calling It's not that I
don't recognize I really do apologize
Ain't it appalling
The procrastinating stalling So slow were almost crawling At
night you'll hear me bawling I'm the pain in your loneliness
I'm the cause of all of your distress Through the time
that we've parted I'm sure your heart has hardened
I admit and do acknowledge this
@gpc

Once YOU know
Your self worth
Don't stop Once YOU know How
worthy you are Never give up
@gpc

If your friends aren't anywhere to be found
When you need them
They aren't friends to begin with
@gpc

You can clone ten million people
To be like you
But you can never clone ten million people
To do as you do
@gpc

If you want someone to be good
Give them the chance to do good
@gpc

Janet Saltzman

Thunder gets my attention
Awaiting the rain is what keeps me there
Lightning is pleasurably blinding
It's the sound
Of the rhythm of the rain When it hits the ground
It's what I like to hear It's a beautiful sound
Everytime I hear it again in the future
That's because its nature
@gpc

Jesus tell me why Of friends I've none I
know fully well You're the only one
@gpc

You pay for a perm
You pay for a tan
$3000 for lips
Even more for an ass
Do you really think you should be racist?
@gpc

Dude, I'm scared
The fighting has just begun
Dude, I'm scared
The fighting is for everyone
@gpc

There is a must
That needs saying
If you can admit your true feelings Amongst
those who judge you Then you are the most
powerful Regardless of what they say
You must remember
Their thoughts and opinions are invalid Why...because their
thoughts and opinions were given to them without validity
@gpc

Be intelligent enough to rise above the
rumors.
@gpc

Society seems to care more about the paycheck
Than the people
@gpc

Livid, Lucid, Lust

There is so much to be remembered
Yet too much to be forgotten
BLM@GPC

If it's a sin to hurt yourself Imagine what
you'll get for hurting somebody else
@gpc

If you are the company you keep Care less about representing
yourself Care more about representing the company
Don't care about with whom you're working with
Care more about whom you're working for
@gpc

There is nothing you need from your exterior
that you cannot obtain from your interior
@gpc

SPELLED with The same

Letters

BEGIN BEING!!

@gpc

When you love the gym and know
the meaning of hard work
The guilt you have to deal with is working or working out
@gpc

To those who think They are

breakingme

You are only making me

@gpc

Janet Saltzman

Those who fly solo

Have the mightiest of wings

@gpc

Only way to avoid being torn apart

Is to lead with your head

Instead of your heart

@gpc

Janet Saltzman

Sex is taken out of context And just like
religion We've made a mess
Making new rules along the way
For those of us who bi-sexual, bi-curious or gay
@gpc

Relax, relate, release put your mind
at ease Please do as you feel
But please feel as you do
@gpc

Janet Saltzman

When you commence to have sex
What's going on in your head? Sometimes, it's of
the others request Realistically, most just think
of themselves It makes a big difference
Think of the other's preference
@gpc

Frightening to me Someone so genuine Or am I blind to see
Given support, or so I believe Distraught I
am, because My thoughts increase
@gpc

Janet Saltzman

What did I find this time
Could it be someone so sublime Are they too good
for truth; but why? Wait! I think, til days end
Something broken, torn or missing again?
Oops! More wasted time
Lingering in my mind
I'm supposed to find it in myself
Not within someone else
Same mistake again, am I insane?
@gpc

To reveal what we've found to be different
Can be so profound
It's taken as a compliment
@gpc

Tell them how good they feel
Then ask if they like it
@gpc

Talking is good when having sex
Even if it's the same words all the time
Pay attention to what is said
That's how you'll know what they like
@gpc

Janet Saltzman

The end result of sex
Is not the destination
It is the journey to the end
Which is the real sensation
@gpc

Communication is most important
When it comes to interacting with others Sexual
interaction is what you can communicate to the others
That makes it important
@gpc

Variations of sex is one thing Variations of
how you have sex Is just as important
@gpc

Don't have to be religious
To scream "Oh God"
@gpc

When your partner tells you
Their sexual fantasy Don't think that
it's easy Take that opportunity
To make their fantasy a reality
@gpc

Why me?
Isn't that what we ask
Do we?
Even understand when we are in love
Why does it hurt so much?
Ask love why
It consumes our lives
@gpc

The best things in life are free
But we're too busy paying to see
@gpc

If you never experience it
You won't miss it
If you've never tried it How do you know Some people's fears
Are some people's fantasies
@gpc

If you can regress in sex What you
did before You will not miss
If you're in love, That is
@gpc

If you want to make a person orgasism Follow the
moans and the groans But only use it once in a while
So the position doesn't go out of style
@gpc

If you expect it
You won't get it
The journey is your to explore
Yours to enjoy more
@gpc

When it come to sex Everyone's trying to Go with the flow
But sometimes you have to lead instead of follow
@gpc

It clouds the judgement
When men think with the wrong head
And nothing gets accomplished When women talk
with the wrong lips When they're horny anything
you say Will be received in a different way
It's taken as an indication
Towards a subject
You hadn't even mentioned
@gpc

If you ain't playing
With leather vests and chains
You've not seen Where others have been Sex is like medicine
It can relieve much tension
@gpc

If you don't go down
Get out of town
If you don't give face
You're out of the race
@gpc

Your pleasure is my command then
spend the whole night proving it
@gpc

Janet Saltzman

Tell your partner what you love about them
And how good they feel before you touch them
@gpc

Let us all make ourselves up with lashes
It releases us from all our attaches
It's like a playdate and a hey date on our pay date
@gpc

If you're going to say something nasty
Please make it naughty but nice
If you're going to saying something disgusting
Please make it delightfully, delicious If you're going to
say something sleazy Please make it sensual and sexy

There's two ways to work around
Positions you worry about
A way to improve The sound you get Is with sex9
@gpc

If you keep an open mind You'll never what
you'll walk in to And what you'll find
@gpc

Communication is most important When it
comes to, interacting with others Sexual interaction
is what you can communicate to the other
That makes it important
@gpc

Janet Saltzman

Shield round your heart
But don't make it out of concrete
So you can care Make it out of gyprock So the pain you feel
Is easy to bare

When your partner tells you their sexual
fantasy
You might not accept it But please don't reject
You must remind yourself If not you,
Your partner could be telling someone else
Speaking of someone else There's two in a relationship
So don't think of yourself Think of their needs
Or you'll find yourself alone
If you only think of your own
@gpc

Taking sexual mental notes
Would be wise In order to keep Your love life alive
Something for you to use on your own
Take mental notes of the moans and groans
Something to do before, during, and after
Is of what they like
What would make their heart beat faster
If you find it a task Because you're too
shy to ask Then leave it alone
And follow the moans and groans
@gpc

If you're on the receiving end
Start with a compliment About what
they do, How they do it,
And they will do it again Use the time
you spend To explore other things
@gpc

Janet Saltzman

Leaving the bed out of it
Is something new for the both of you
@gpc

Valentine's day is just like any other day
To make up for what we should be doing everyday
@gpc

When you get great sex appreciate it
Some people have to pay for it
@gpc

Everyone wants to be in love
But we're afraid to get hurt
When we wear our hearts on our sleeves
Someone brings the shirt to the laundry

Being in the room with one you can trust
Sexually conversating is a simulating must Sometimes feel
the need to squeeze or touch Those who can be very discreet
Naked of half naked, if need be Can be total eroticism
to the extreme Sharing this with your partner
Can be an optimal sexual starter
@gpc

Nothing is something to do
But you're better than nothing
Nothing is perfect
And so are you
I hear you breathing And that's something I
hear your silence And that ain't nothing
It's something better to do
@gpc

Just because you didn't get laid
It's not for us to say
@gpc

Why do women like being on top during sex
Cause they love to watch a man
Fuck up
@gpc

Janet Saltzman

A bit of advice
No matter what your vice If your on the bottom Fuck up
@gpc

Ooh, It' so good
U feel, U must, & U should
U know, U can, & U could
U wait, U want, & U would
2 much, 2 keep, 2 yourself
2 share, 2 show someone else
@gpc

Janet Saltzman

To R2 my Australian bird
How are you
I can hear you But I can't see you Even
in the light You aren't in sight
But I can feel you here
In my atmosphere

Much depression
From suppression Much Degradation From
Frustration Much obsession From possession
No satisfaction From lack of action
@gpc

Janet Saltzman

I'm young enough to do the splits
And old enough to know the difference
@gpc

Once you get turned on enough
You'll never know
How far you go
What you do when you get there
Only you and I will know
@gpc

We all know
Men think with the wrong head
Women talk too much
Cause they've got too many lips
@gpc

To all of those
Who like to rob the cradle Stop trying
to pull down The pull-ups
@gpc

If they get a shot in the mid-section
Just say let me kiss your boo boo
@gpc

In sex, its not
Head to toe Its toe to head Because you lick up
@gpc

Printed in the United States
by Baker & Taylor Publisher Services